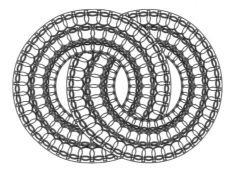

HER KIND

HER KIND

CINDY VEACH

CAVANKERRY
PRESS

CavanKerry Press Ltd.
Fort Lee, New Jersey
www.cavankerrypress.org

Publisher's Cataloging-In-Publication Data
(Prepared by The Donohue Group, Inc.)
Names: Veach, Cindy, author.
Title: Her kind / Cindy Veach.
Description: First edition. | Fort Lee, New Jersey : CavanKerry
   Press, 2021. | Includes bibliographical references.
Identifiers: ISBN 9781933880877
Subjects: LCSH: Women—Poetry. | Witches—Poetry. | Victims—
   Poetry. | Trials (Witchcraft)—Massachusetts—Salem—Poetry.
   | Salem (Mass.)—History—Colonial period, ca. 1600-1775—
   Poetry. | United States—Politics and government—21st century—
   Poetry. | LCGFT: Poetry.
Classification: LCC PS3622.E33 H47 2021 | DDC 811/.6—dc23

Cover artwork: io. Lagana/Flickr.com
Cover and interior text design by Ryan Scheife, Mayfly Design
First Edition 2021, Printed in the United States of America

CAVANKERRY
PRESS

Made possible by funds from the
New Jersey State Council on the Arts, a partner
agency of the National Endowment for the Arts.

In addition, CavanKerry Press gratefully acknowledges generous
emergency support received during the COVID-19 pandemic
from the following funders:

Community of Literary Magazines and Presses

New Jersey Arts and Culture Recovery Fund

New Jersey Council for the Humanities

New Jersey Economic Development Authority

Northern New Jersey Community Foundation

The Poetry Foundation

US Small Business Administration

Also by Cindy Veach

Gloved Against Blood (2017)
Innocents (2020)

for my sisters

A woman like that is misunderstood.

—Anne Sexton

Contents

I, Witch

So what if I woke up changed   it's not like I'm a wild hog
or some Evill thing   not a Reall hog
that follows you home   *Jumps into the window*
a *Munky* with *Cocks feete w'th Claws*   don't believe
what my Accuser says   or believe it
the fact is   my divorce attorney's building
sits on the site of the prison   where they kept the Accused
in Chaines   in 1692   I came there with a silk scarf
worn loosely   at the neck   borders looped
with colored thread   he came with daisies   dark
chocolate   and proclaimed
my wife came towards me and found fault with me
downstairs   in the dungeon   they chained us to the walls
to keep our spirits from escaping   *in the Liknes of a bird*

3

Rose of Jericho

I'm not sure about this gift. This tangle
of dried roots curled into a fist. This gnarl

I've let sit for weeks beside the toaster
and cookbooks on a bed of speckled granite.

What am I waiting for? Online I find
Rose of Jericho spells and rituals for safe birth,

well-being, warding off the evil eye.
At first I thought I'd buy some white stones,

a porcelain bowl. But I didn't and I didn't.
I don't believe in omens. This still fist

of possibility all wrapped up in itself.
There it sat through the holidays, into the new year.

Through all the days I've been gone. Dormant.
But today, in an inch of water,

out of curiosity, I awakened
the soul of Jericho. Limb by limb it unfolded

and turned moss green. It reminded me
of the Northwest, its lush undergrowth,

how twice despite the leaden clouds,
the rain, I found happiness there.

From tumbleweed to lush fern flower,
reversible, repeatable. And what am I

to make of this? Me, this woman who doesn't
believe. Doesn't take anything on faith. I won't

let it rot. I'll monitor the water level. Keep the mold
at bay. I tend things, but I do not pray.

Spectral Evidence

Because she said she saw
    and therefore

these pinholes in her skin
    on one arm to be exact—

look how they crisscross
    make a doily of the flesh—

and because she said she saw
    you not you

take a small pin
    from your pocket

a straight pin
    with a flat head

and because she said it was
    it was

therefore you
    therefore not a dream

puncturing each pore
    you in the flesh not flesh

with a common pin—

Elizabeth Howe of Sorrows

Hanged, 1692

I had to be my husband's eyes—

        the light

that could not reach them—

        leading him about by the hand

tilling the land my father gave me

        running the household

        and for this

they would not let me

        com into the church of Ipswich

        and for this

they said I bewitched horses, cows, sows

        and *was the cause*

        of sorows

that killed the Perley's

        little Hannah.

No, never in all my life . . .

        I saw

I had to be the husband—

        eyes, mouth, muscle—

        and took the lead

and hanged for it.

I Have Seen Women Manipulate Men with Just a Twitch of Their Eye

Sarah Wildes, Hanged, 1692

Of course, the crimson scarf—
     worn loosely at the neck

colorful and coy. Of course,
     the deceased first wife's sister—

neighbor, accuser.
     Of course, the dispute

over the Topsfield/Salem line—
     John Wildes, surveyor (and spouse).

Of course, her gruffness
     but at the same time

her beauty. Also—
     too great intimacy

with one Thomas Wardell of Ipswich,
     although neither was married

at the time. And, of course, the whipping—
     for fornication.

Of course, too forward (wild)
     in her youth.

And glamorous (in her youth).
     That too.

Rebecca Nurse of the Accused

Hanged, 1692

At first the jury returned *not Guilty*
to which the judge said

retire and reconsider
the *not.*

After all she had not answered
the question she had not heard—

guilty of being hard of hearing
maybe mouthing

what?

Guilty of having a temper—
arguing with neighbors.

Guilty too of piety—
thirty-nine attesting

to her deep devotion.
Still, The Afflicted swore

it was her apparition
that did the *pinchings*

and *prickings* of their flesh.
And in court, when she raised her arms,

The Afflicted raised their arms.
And when she inclined her head,

The Afflicted inclined their heads.

In the Snare of the Devil

I tell myself
My name is fault and blame
I tell myself
This is just noise
I tell myself
My name is fault and blame and home-wrecker
I tell myself
Stop it
I tell myself
My name is fault and blame and home-wrecker and bitch
I tell myself
Shut up
I tell myself
My name is fault and blame and home-wrecker and bitch
    and witch
I tell myself
Enough
I tell myself
Go back home head in hand holding out your sorry tongue
I tell myself
Resist

Resist
I tell myself
Go back home head in hand holding out your sorry tongue
I tell myself
Enough
I tell myself
My name is fault and blame and home-wrecker and bitch
    and witch
I tell myself

Shut up
I tell myself
My name is fault and blame and home-wrecker and bitch
I tell myself
Stop it
I tell myself
My name is fault and blame and home-wrecker
I tell myself
This is just noise
I tell myself
My name is fault and blame
I tell myself

You Are Witnessing the Single Greatest Witch Hunt in American Political History

Martha Corey, Hanged, 1692

It's true my husband testified against me
because of the ointment & the sick mutt,
the hipped ox & that night he saw me
kneel down to the harth, as if at prayr, but
heard nothing. In the end he refused to
speak out against me, but when those
Children cryed there was a yellow bird who
suckled my fingers, the judges deposed
me—*What bird was that the children spoke of?*
What bird was it? The devil did not take
my *shape & hurt these.* I know nothing of
this yellow bird or witchery. My mistake?
I bore an illegitimate child—Benoni, son
of my sorrow & dearly loved one.

Dear Moon

You appear halved tonight—
    darkness your camouflage,

chameleon, cover-up—
    and when he says

I was only half there
    I look up to you

hanging
    in the skylight—

even eclipsed,
    half full, halfway,

you are not a fraction.
    Nothing is ever missing.

You are not a part, a slice,
    hangnail, sliver, morsel,

crescent, quarter, waning,
    or halfhearted.

You are sum,
    whole, all there—

Contradiction Express

I was bamboozled
by love notes
left in pockets, duffels, shoes.

I went along,
could not resist
his lexicon.

One for me. One for him.
A three-decade quid pro quo.
I wish there were a bibliography

that cited every fight.
First a ripe tomato.
Then a fist. Both hit

the wall, split.
I rode that coaster.
Hung on for dear life.

Love note. Bloodlust.
Love note. Bloodlust.

At the Threshold

Salem Witch Trials Tercentenary Memorial

Slabs of worn stone, inscribed

> *For my life now lies in your hands*

Gray slabs that do not touch

> *On my dying day, I am no witch*

Where their words slide under

> *If I would confess i should save my life*

Midsentence

> *I do plead not guilty*

Before the mute tombstones

> *God knows I am innocent*

Where the tourists mill

> *I am wholly innocent of such wickedness*

And pose for selfies

> *Oh Lord help me*

A Crazed, Crying Lowlife and a Dog

Bridget Bishop, Hanged, 1692

If she has *Sundry peeces of lace*
some of which are so short

you can't *judge them fit for any uce*
their purpose is for poppets

stuck with *headles pins*
w'th the points outward

in holes in cellar walls.
And if, upon examination,

her dried flesh hangs like teats,
it is further proof. Furthermore,

if there's a black pig in her orchard.
Or if a black *creture* follows you home

and *Jumps into the window—*
a *Munky* with *Cocks feete w'th Claws*

and the face somewhat more like a dog's—
if when you strike it there is *noe Substance.*

If she wears a *Red paragon Bodys*
borders looped with colored thread,

quarrels with her husband—
you old rogue, you old devil—

then appears in public bloodied
and bruised, accuse—

I did clearely see s'd Bridget Bushop.
I Espied s'd Bridget Bushop.

Apparition

A charm of starlings at nightfall,

      a whorl of leaves or runes of glass

in a kaleidoscope divining a squall

      of starlings at nightfall,

shape-shifting cauldron of wings, pall

      of specters swirling en masse,

a spell of starlings at nightfall,

      a whorl of leaves or runes of glass.

Blessed Teresa of Calcutta Declared a Saint before a Huge Crowd at the Vatican

Samia Shahid, Strangled, 2016

Today there is a new saint and Samia is strangled.
With her scarf wound round and round Samia is strangled.

Her father tricked her into coming back to Punjab.
She wore her blue scarf home and was strangled.

Some say Mother Teresa didn't deserve sainthood—she
Helped the dying die. Yet, Samia deserved to be strangled?

Her father feigned illness so she'd return. She came home
Wearing her beautiful scarf and was strangled.

Her ex-husband raped her for marrying another.
For marrying for love Samia was raped and strangled.

How can there be a saint without a God Almighty?
She prayed to him, came to him, only to be strangled.

Margaret Scott of Children Lost

Hanged, 1692

I knocked on doors. Asked
    for coins for corn.
        Each time I thought

I could not
    but each time hunger
        stole my tongue—

Please, may I *gleane* corn
    in your *felld?* Daniel Wycomb, you would not
        part with any ears.

Guilt, not me, is the reason
    that ye oxen would not goe forward:
        but backward with the load of corn.

Look at me—
    a widow for so long
        I've forgotten his face

but not the faces
    of every child I lost.
        They say I lost too many

and must hang
    for this and *sundry other Acts*
        of Witchcraft.

Reasons You Might Have Been
Accused of Being a Witch in 1692

You are a woman. You are middle-aged.
You have an extra nipple, mole, freckle
(or basically any other mark on your body).
You stumble over your words.

You have an extra nipple, mole, freckle.
When asked to say a prayer
you stumble over the words.
You are married but don't have children.

When asked to say a prayer
you are the envy of other people.
You are married but don't have enough children.
You associate with someone suspected of witchcraft.

You are the envy of other people.
You are perceived as bitchy.
You associate with someone suspected of witchcraft.
Your milk spoiled.

You are perceived as bitchy.
You are of low status.
Your milk spoiled
(or anything vaguely negative happened to or around you).

You are of low status.
You have any mark on your body.
Your milk spoiled.
You are a woman. You are middle-aged.

Tornado Warning

When I think about it now, I am fearless
but sometimes I still hear

the hum of our minivan coming back from Iowa City—
that two-lane highway with too many white crosses—
troopers flagging us down, ordering us to lie

belly down in the ditch. Iowa sky. Imperial sky.
Every spiny tendril that drops from a dark cloud
reminds me of the bed fear made. Silence meant trouble,

a brewing. I prayed for thunder. I welcomed the cackle
of lightning, rages, yelling matches—

but a sudden drop in pressure, the sucking out
of sound. I got good at seeing it coming—

sky purpling, moving over our house,
our house slanting into shadow.

I went down to the cellar to weather
each storm. Tornados are cruel.
Of course, I had to leave him.

Ogre

Having come to a field having come
      to a creek in a field having
            come to seek out the beast

in the knee of the field by the creek
      the beast that lives in my field
         by my creek

having come to this apogee
      without a bead of belief
         in the hour of my need

having come in the hour of my need
      to my field by my creek
         and found him

in my field by my creek
      having come and refused
         to get down on my knees

in my field by my creek
      having come having refused him
         come now Circe disarm him

Our Lady of Perpetual Compassion

Ann Pudeator, Hanged, 1692

Because you asked them to stay mum
none of your five children
came to your defense

even though they knew
you didn't visit the sick
pretending kindnes

and kill. What nurse can make
every patient well? They knew the poppets
stuck with thorns were placed

on purpose and all the ointments—
you put them in so many things—
were for concocting twenty kinds

of soap. They would have said
you weren't the *caus of Jno Turners falling*
off the cherry tree. You had nothing

to do with the *pinching & Bruseing* of John Best's wife
Till her Earms & other parts of her Body Looked Black
and that you would never have forced Sarah

to *sett her hand to the book.* Samuel Pikworth swore
you passed him *as swifte as if a burd flue by*
but if you could have bewitched yourself into a bird

you would have. Instead, you stood and stated
what your children knew—the *Evidence* against you
was *altogether false & untrue.*

Pretending Kindness

The day our mattress morphed
    into the mattress he pressed

        down on me

my body folded
    fetal. Some things are not

        meant to be forgotten.

Hot fire of a snapped
    wrist. Taking the fight outside

        so we wouldn't wake

the kids. Busted anyway
    because they heard a fisher

        cat, which is not a cat

but a weasel, murdering
    in the dark

        each vicious scream stabbing

the dead of night.
    I meant to keep quiet

        just between me and the cracked

scaphoid the X-ray kept missing.
    Some things are better off not said

        or said slant—

either way I pay
  and pay some more.

I, Kikimora

The spider first classified
the year I wed—

spider smaller than a speck
of straw, spider of the bog

of swamp, wetland, marsh, quagmire.
A mere wisp of khaki chaff, of hair,

a sphinx moth, night butterfly, invisible
wraith who slips through the keyhole

after dark—both beautiful and ugly,
whiny, glass half-empty noisemaker,

dish breaker, home-wrecker—
wet footprints across his heart.

Oomancy Triggers Witch Hunt

Because albumen in water
      shape-shifts,

becomes bells, fingers, spires,
      becomes omen—

a future husband, his occupation
      but also, unexpectedly,

a *spectre in the likeness of a coffin*,
      a sign of *diabolical molestation*—

Elizabeth and Abigail
      fell into fake fits

barking like dogs, complaining
      invisible spirits were pinching them—

therefore The Afflicted,
      therefore The Accused.

Mary of the Blessed Innocent

Mary Ayer Parker, Hanged, 1692

It is written that her touch alone
recovered the afflicted out of their fitts.

And there was that black hog,
or some Evill thing not a Reall hog,

that chased home Old Man Westgate,
openmouthed, as if it *would have*

devoured me att thatt Instant. He said
he had determined in his mind

it was Mary Parker.
Also, William Barker Jr. confessed

she *went w'th him to Afflict Martha Sprauge*
and that she *rod Upon a pole*

and was baptized at 5 Mile pond,
but to this day there's speculation

that the teenage girls who accused her
meant another Mary Parker—

distemper of the mind Mary Stevens Parker
or sister-in-law Mary Markstone Parker

or possibly niece Mary Parker
but, most likely, the scandalous,

twice-convicted of fornication
and mother of an illegitimate child

Mary Parker of Salem Town
instead of the hanged Mary Ayer Parker.

Still, Mary, Mary, Mary, Mary, or Mary—

I, Circe

I love swine. It's all I have to show
for my years on the isle of Iowa.

I like swine made out of anything—
flesh, glass, stone, fabric, porcelain.

I even count a low-fire, glazed-in-gold
warthog in my collection. The male artist,

a transplant from Mill Valley, titled it *Farm Art*
like an aesthetic dig at the heartland,

at the neighbor lady who taught me
to make kolaches with prune filling,

at the boy who was my first,
who could dock the tails

of piglets in his sleep
and two-hand an electric fence.

Sometimes I crave that Grant Wood land
not flat, not flat at all, but I can't go back.

Is that why I keep adding to my stash?
Swine ornaments dangle from light fixtures,

cabinets. Swine tea towels, pitchers, butter
dishes, pull toy, corkscrew, talisman.

He Damaged Me

Alone in a boat
The Damaged hugs

The shoreline
Lest the waters rise

And anyway the birds.
How the heron hides.

Her indigo plumage
Patient beyond measure.

//

In a wood
The Damaged walks

The same path,
An out and back.

Nervous vole,
Hungry hawk.

And always the empty
Air.

//

At the city hotel
The Damaged stays

In her room.
Harbor view. Sailboats

Race to the mark.
Tack back.

But also
Sharks.

//

All night
The Damaged speaks

To Alexa.
Streams.

Thin skin.
She touches herself

Down there.
Bleeds.

//

Alright,
The Damaged says.

Or has no opinion.
No favorite

Dish, décor, place,
Color—

Though once
Red.

//

In a car, speeding,
The Damaged opens

The door.
Ditch blur. Its clot

Of clover. While
All the whitetails

On the shoulder bravely
Flicker and flee.

No Collusion

Wilmott Redd, Hanged, 1692

Local fishermen knew her as Mammy,
wife of Marblehead County of Essex
fisherman Samuel Redd. Cranky
and poor she had only rags for dresses.
"Witch," accused a neighbor after a dispute
over butter. It didn't help that her
daughter was once married to that brute
George Burroughs, who many liked to refer
to as *ringleader* of the witches.
Mary, Mercy, Abigail fell into fits,
and Ann swore she brought her the Book. Bitches!
When asked were they *Bewitcht*? She kept her wits.
All she would say was: my opinion
is they are in sad condition.

Wife/Witch

Alice Parker, Hanged, 1692

I've searched high and low and still all I know
is that you were *but a simple housewife*
married to a fisherman, *a woman of faith*
and good deeds. I want you to know
everything your accusers affirmed
under oath to the Jury of Inquest—
the book brought: *to siign*
the needle into the Poppit
choking: them & squeezing them
death of Tho Wastgate: and crew: that was foundred in the sea
death of goodwife ormes her son that was drown'd
Michael Chapmans Death in Boston harbour—
was duly documented, transcribed, archived, scrutinized,
and determined to be irrefutably all lies.

In Search Of

It's all over the news. Scientists have discovered
        an incirrate, or unfinned octopod,

also described as an undescribed species,
        while searching the waters

off the Hawaiian Islands near Necker Island—
        its suckers in one row on each arm,

a pale white, billowy body with black eyes,
        a ghost creature, the deepest dwelling

octopod ever found,
        a surprise while plumbing

the depths—
        I've been scared to death my whole life:

the girl who crept into her parents' bedroom
        convinced her hysterical heart

was galloping toward the finish line. I'm fluent
        in fear. Be Safe is my mantra.

It's as if there's a flashing red light
        on my head—the Siren who *saves*

ships from the rocks. I'm a total failure
        at risk. Like the time I went five miles over

and a cop came out of nowhere
        license and registration. Or when I

rebelled as a teen and OD'd on Blue Meanies.
        And how was I supposed to know

that my palpitations, after the man
        at Stop & Shop seized, was a panic attack?

Can you blame me for dropping
        my groceries and running all the way home?

For becoming instantly agoraphobic? Hello, death
        at my door. It's been a lifetime of crossing

on *Walk*, annual checkups, sensible
        shoes, swimming only in pools, killing

every spider. This is why I stayed married
        and stayed married, decades of eggshells

and gaslighting. But now, because of this bewitching
        specter at the bottom of the Pacific,

I'm getting up my gumption.
        What else is left to do?

My air is running out. I've been waiting
        for my heart to stop long enough.

What the hell. It's settled.
        Let the panic rush in.

Let it course through me.
        I'm going down there. Alone.

Such a Nasty Woman

Susannah Martin, Hanged, 1692

Call me troublemaker.
I speak my mind.
I have a temper.
Call me witch: Mary, Abigail, Mercy, Ann.
Bear witness: William, John, Bernard, Thomas,
Reverend Cotton Mather—and I quote:
This woman was one of the most impudent,
scurrilous, wicked creatures of this world.
Therefore—
take me away. Search
with your cold hands
until my flesh seizes up—
in the morning her nipples
were found to be full
as if the milk would come—
fingers fingering, eyes eyeing
looking, looking
for the extra teat
to suckle my imps—
but later in the day
her breasts were slack,
as if milk had already been given
to someone or something . . .
Go ahead. Search me twice.
Twice, no witch's teat.
Therefore.
Cart me away.
Gallows me.
Pity my poor imps.

Woman Climbs Statue of Liberty
in Protest

Therese Patricia Okoumou, Guilty of Trespassing, 2018

She said, I climb to protest our nation's "zero
tolerance" immigration policy. She said, I climb
to abolish ICE. They said, trespasser. They said,
disorderly conduct. When she sat on the skirts
of Lady Liberty, we watched them climb
after her. They said, get down. Our hero
said, *I'm not discouraged.* She made her bed.
And we watched and cheered and put a curse
on those who wanted to arrest her
for protesting putting children into cages.
Oh yes, we witches watched her carry our truth
up and over that ledge like a beautiful sooth-
sayer, strong and lithe. Goodbye Dark Ages.
We climb with her. We climb with her.

Practice the Spell: Divorce

Load a tumbler
with ice to the brim.
Spank those fat rectangles
from your grandmother's pastel-coloured ice tray—

where her fingers stuck, so too should yours.
Add tap water until it fills the gaps
between each cube—
take it as cold as it can come

and still pass down your throat.
Repeat after me:
"Please hurt my teeth. Leak into the places
where the enamel is weak. Hurt me."

Eight eight-ounce glasses every day
until your heart goes numb
until you can stand in front of him
and say that cold word cold.

I Filed for Divorce and Sundry Other Acts of Witchcraft Therefore

I am the earthquake and its tectonic plate.
A rock chucked into a languid lake.
I am the headache that keeps you awake.
An unexpected snake at the end of the rake.
A rock tossed into a placid lake.
I am the shake that rattles the gate
and the faux pas that deflates the cake.
A rock dropped into a flat lake.
I am a plague outbreak.
The thirst you can't slake.
A rock flung into a tranquil lake
and the rip in something opaque.
I am the damn stake in the landscape.
The firebreak that forsakes.
A rock cast into a still lake.
The mean old drake.
The keepsake that's fake.
A rock hurled into a serene lake.
The cause of your toothache
and the failed windbreak.
Every mistake.
A rock pitched into a quiet lake.
I am the one to hate.
No one's namesake.
The earthquake and its tectonic plate.

I, Chedipe

Hide-and-seek placenta—
gully washer, dream stopper
bleeding out
on cold tile—
and me
holding the clot
in both hands
saying *look*
I am undead
now I can suck the life
out of men.

What Bird Was That

I wake up to a bird calling *cheat, cheat, cheat.*
       What bird are you and whom do you call?

You caught me sleeping
       with the windows open.

What sounds like footsteps in the woods—
       squirrels scurrying through dead leaves.

Things are not what they seem.
       When will new leaves arrive?

There is no one here.
       The greening has begun—

Did I leave you? Say, *no*
       more, no more.

What season is it? What sky dare
       be so blue? And why those words?

Spring comes despite you,
       little cheat. Nest builder. Nest builder.

Where are you? Your hungry ones are coming
       shrouded in shell. Speak up. Tell.

For Leaving

After miles of his words
coming at me

over the Bluetooth
I pass a haymow

close to the road.
One cow lying down.

Lying against it. One
upright, grazing.

One measured word
after the other

he makes his case
against me

in the name of his love.
I notice

the soft-bristled hair
above their lips,

how round their eyes are
and I want to say

doe-like
as I fight hard

not to say
what I've always said.

Oh lovely calm cows
in the muddy snow

beside a hill of hay
that makes its own heat.

Watching the News in My Attorney's Waiting Room

They're burning Harry Potter books in Poland.
It felt like magic when I gave him my hand.

        It was magic when I gave him my hand
        And the justice pronounced us husband and wife.

I was pregnant and wanted to be his wife.
They're livestreaming the bonfire of books.

        Priests and altar boys burning "wicked" books.
        In my country divorce is legal

And books about magic aren't evil.
But if I file for divorce I'm a bitch.

        But if I file for divorce I'm a witch.
        There doesn't need to be a reason.

There doesn't need to be a good reason.
They're burning Harry Potter books in Poland.

I Don't Know, I Don't Know

Sarah Good, Hanged, 1692

Sarah Good, what evil
spirit have you? None. Have
you? No. Why
do you? I do not. Who
do you? I am falsely. Why
did you? I did not. Have
you? No. Sarah
Good, do you not see? I do
not. Who do you? No-
body. How? What
do I know? Who
was it? I do not know. Who?
It was. What is it you say?
If I must tell. Do
tell. If I must tell
I will tell. It is. What?
If I must tell I will
tell. It is. Who?
god. What God?
The god.

Poem the Day After Kavanaugh Is Confirmed to the Highest Court in the Land

When it's 76 degrees in October in New England,
I consider it a reprieve, a bonus, a gold coin
to slip in my pocket and I put all else aside,
go for a walk, reveling in snippets
of conversation, baseball and football games
spilling from windows opened wide
and when I reach the sea that plashes away no matter what,
I cheer an old couple that go for a swim
but inside I know this is the cusp of the end
of light, of warmth and though my eyes want to hold
the still blooming daisies, the widemouthed dahlias
that I pass on my way home
and though I spare them the terrible news
my mind's eye sees only brown stalks, spent flowers.

Gallows Hill Project Team Verifies Site of Salem Witch Trial Hangings

Near the stoplight. By the big Walgreens.
Over to the right. See that rock ledge?
Where it's dark. Those bare oak trees.
Near the stoplight. By the big Walgreens
And the Dunkin' Donuts full of randy teens.
Now we know. It's not where legend said.
But near the stoplight. By the big Walgreens.
Over to the right. That rock ledge.

The Witch Dungeon Museum

Here, you will find the truth
has morphed into yet another tourist trap—a tour
through a low-budget movie set where uncouth
locals reenact the trials before a jury of poor,
unblinking, aging mannequins.
Downstairs, in the basement
dungeon, you're in for more sad shenanigans—
sagging dummies being flogged and bent
in two while the witch, just convicted upstairs,
on cue, shrills and jumps out—*Boo!*
Total veracity is guaranteed—all signage bears
a quintessential witch silhouette, a déjà vu
of Halloween candy wrappers—please, dear Tourist,
keep in mind there were never any witches here.

Trump Has Called the Investigation a Witch Hunt 84 Times

Martha Carrier, Hanged, 1692

They said she brought smallpox to Andover.
They said she killed her father and brother
making her *a Queen in Hell,* aka Landowner.
Neighbors testified it was none other
than Goody Carrier who haunted
them at night. They said she bit Sue Sheldon
threatening to cut her throat because she wanted
her to sign the book. She stuck a pin in dumb
Ann Putnam. Killed Samuel Preston's cow
for being *very Lusty.* And there was that
devil *man wispering in her ear.* Somehow
she caused the death of Allen Toothaker's cat.
For these Complaints, though each one was a lie,
she was condemned *by the Grace of God* to die.

You've Got to Deny, Deny, and Push
Back on These Women

A woman's adultery is a very serious attack on the
honor and dignity of a man.

—Judge Neto de Moura of the Porto Court of Appeals

And still they pick up a stone. And still they throw a stone.
Because the woman. The woman.

Mr. Judge. The Honorable. Sets him free.
After all, his honor. Infinite

these one-sided stones
though John wrote what Jesus said—

how no one touched a stone.
And still they pick up a stone. And still they throw a stone.

Because asking for it. She was asking.
She was the cause.

Because of clothes
on her body clothesline

in a spring breeze. Golden sunshine.
Fresh. So fresh.

Because not a dedicated wife.
Not, not, not.

Jesus spoke. John wrote.
No one touched a stone.

And still they pick up a stone. And still they throw a stone.
Because the woman. The woman deserved it.

Obstruction of Justice

Mary Easty, Hanged, 1692

They said she hurt them and *brought them the Book*
& then they fell into fits. When Mary's hands
are *clincht together,* they point, cry out—Look!
Mercy Lewis's hands are *clincht.* When Mary stands
with her head bowed—*put up her head, for while*
her head is bowed the necks of these are broken.
She petitions twice. First, for a fair trial—
Judge, please be of councell to us. Again,
already condemned, she begs—*your honor*
please examine *theis Aflicted Persons*
strictly and keepe them apart. This wife, mother,
sister, her *appointed time sett,* certain,
pleads not for her own life but that instead
no more Innocentt blood may be shed.

Taylor Swift Makes *Forbes's* Most Powerful Women List

A WHOLE WITCH RITUALLLLL I LOVE YOU TAYLOR A SWIFT.

Shake off the haters. Here's to savvy, broomsticks, red lipstick.

She's giving me major Scarlet Witch vibes & I am HERE. FOR. IT.

A WHOLE WITCH RITUALLLLL I LOVE YOU TAYLOR A SWIFT.

I wanted to hug her when she started pointing to herself, raised a fist—

"they're burning all the witches even if you aren't one." Here's to witch grit.

A WHOLE WITCH RITUALLLLL I LOVE YOU TAYLOR A SWIFT.

Shake off the haters. Here's to savvy, broomsticks, red lipstick.

Spell

When is leaving justified?
One part eggshell to two parts love?
Two parts eggshell to one part love?

My head is full of noise.
My head is a hung jury.
My head is a congregation

seated on hardwood benches
while outside the Chinese maple
is ablaze and deserves a sidelong glance.

I cast my eyes knowing
I could not look back.
Those leaves escaping

the tree, sparking the air,
made me think
of lightning bugs

when I hadn't thought
of lightning bugs
since Bloomington

since the rental on Bender Road.
I raced my sisters
across that dark yard.

I wanted to capture
all the light.
It wasn't a secret.

There were people
who drove down our road at night
to dump unwanted puppies.

How could they do that?
And yet.
How could I?

He Punishes Me with Flowers

Knowing they're my favorite,

he brings

red gerberas to the settlement meeting.

Guilt schleps them back to my apartment.

Guilt places them in the living room.

I can barely look at them

on the borrowed coffee table.

Watch how I avert my eyes

when I walk by.

I decide to help them die.

Withhold water. Resist

investigating the stems

for telltale signs of rot.

They were scarlet.

Now they're darker. They're dried-

up blood. They sit there

and insinuate.

Settlement

Ranch houses on a cul-de-sac.
Tents pitched under I-5
or the Fremont Bridge,
but also an agreement.

For instance,
a document that divides.
Opposite of
what's mine is yours
what's yours is mine.

To settle as in dust
and sediment
but also
to agree to agree.

I, Hecate

Between Queen, Liminal Sorceress,
Crossroads Guardian—
story of my life.

Who are you today, my ex would taunt.
More than just a Gemini,
a *trimorphos*, human form in triplicate:

birth, love, death
maiden, mother, crone
moon, earth, underworld

I'll take triplicity
over duplicity any day.
Three heads are better

even if one
has to be a dog—
a bitch:

dog, dog, dog
dog, serpent, horse
dog, cow, boar.

Even if it means
I am witch—
that old crone at the cauldron

stirring willows, dark yew, blackthorn.
It took a torch, a key, a dagger
to cut away a past.

It took thirty years.
It took
all three of me.

Notes

The University of Virginia's Salem Witch Trials Documentary Archive and Transcription Project (http://salem.lib. virginia.edu/home.html), which includes the verbatim transcriptions of the Salem Witch Trial court records, became the primary source for the italicized quotations throughout the collection. Spelling inconsistencies and errors found in the original court records are preserved.

The title *Her Kind* is from the Anne Sexton poem "Her Kind."

Hecate's Wheel, also known as the Stropholos of Hecate, is an ancient Greek symbol used to represent the moon goddess Hecate. "Hecate's Wheel Symbol—Origins and Meaning," Symbolsage: Understanding the World through Symbols and Mythology, https://symbolsage.com/hecate-wheel-symbolism-and-meaning/.

"I, Witch" quotes (in italics) are from Salem Witch Trials Documentary Archive and Transcription Project, http:// salem.lib.virginia.edu/n97.html, http://salem.lib.virginia.edu/ n13.html, http://salem.lib.virginia.edu/n37.html, http://salem. lib.virginia.edu/n87.html.

"Elizabeth Howe of Sorrows" quotes (in italics) and inspiration are from Salem Witch Trials Documentary Archive and Transcription Project, http://salem.lib.virginia.edu/n72.html.

"I Have Seen Women Manipulate Men with Just a Twitch of Their Eye" quotes (in italics) and inspiration are from "The 'Witches' of Salem, Massachusetts," https://www.legends ofamerica.com/ma-witches/. Title attributed to Donald Trump.

"Rebecca Nurse of the Accused" quotes (in italics) and inspiration are from Salem Witch Trials Documentary Archive and Transcription Project, http://salem.lib.virginia.edu/n94.html.

"You Are Witnessing the Single Greatest Witch Hunt in American Political History" quotes (in italics) and inspiration are from Salem Witch Trials Documentary Archive and Transcription Project, http://salem.lib.virginia.edu/n38.html#n38.11, http://salem.lib.virginia.edu/n38.html#n38.2. Title attributed to Donald Trump.

"At the Threshhold" quotes (in italics) are from the entryway to the Salem Witch Trials Memorial, which is inscribed with the victims' protests as documented in court records.

"A Crazed, Crying Lowlife and a Dog" quotes (in italics) and inspiration are from Salem Witch Trials Documentary Archive and Transcription Project, http://salem.lib.virginia.edu/n13.html. See also the sources of "I, Witch." Title attributed to Donald Trump.

"Margaret Scott of Children Lost" quotes (in italics) and inspiration from Salem Witch Trials Documentary Archive and Transcription Project, http://salem.lib.virginia.edu/n119.html.

"Reasons You Might Have Been Accused of Being a Witch in 1692" is a found poem. The source is Lara Rutherford-Morrison, "Would You Have Been Called a Witch in Salem?" *Bustle*, May 3, 2015, https://www.bustle.com/articles/79820-10-reasons-you-might-have-been-accused-of-being-a-witch-in-the-17th-century.

"Our Lady of Perpetual Compassion" quotes (in italics) and inspiration are from Salem Witch Trials Documentary Archive and Transcription Project, http://salem.lib.virginia.edu/n113.html.

"Oomancy Triggers Witch Hunt" quotes (in italics) are from Rebecca Brooks, "Ann Putnam Jr: Villain or Victim?" History of Massachusetts Blog, July 6, 2015, https://historyofmassachusetts.org/ann-putnam-jr/.

"Mary of the Blessed Innocent" quotes (in italics) and inspiration are from Salem Witch Trials Documentary Archive and Transcription Project, http://salem.lib.virginia.edu/n97.html#n97.7, http://salem.lib.virginia.edu/n98.html, http://salem.lib.virginia.edu/n10.html, http://salem.lib.virginia.edu/n10.html#n10.2, and Jacqueline Kelly, "The Untold Story of Mary Ayer Parker: Gossip and Confusion in 1692," June 2005, http://salem.lib.virginia.edu/people/?group.num=all. See also the sources of "I, Witch."

"He Damaged Me" takes its title from the following line from the poem "Epistemology" by Jennifer Chang: "I loved a man for how he damaged me."

"No Collusion" quotes (in italics) and inspiration are from Salem Witch Trials Documentary Archive and Transcription Project, http://salem.lib.virginia.edu/n114.html#n114.4 and http://salem.lib.virginia.edu/letters/to_cotton1.

html. See also source of "I Have Seen Women Manipulate Men with Just a Twitch of Their Eye." Title attributed to Donald Trump.

"Wife/Witch" quotes (in italics) and inspiration are from Salem Witch Trials Documentary Archive and Transcription Project, http://salem.lib.virginia.edu/n97.html #n97.5. See also source of "I Have Seen Women Manipulate Men with Just a Twitch of Their Eye."

"Such a Nasty Woman" quotes (in italics) are from Rebecca Beatrice Brooks, "The Witchcraft Trial of Susannah Martin," History of Massachusetts Blog, February 14, 2012, https://historyofmassachusetts.org/susannah-martin-accused-witch-from-salisbury/. See also source of "I Have Seen Women Manipulate Men with Just a Twitch of Their Eye." Title attributed to Donald Trump.

"Woman Climbs Statue of Liberty in Protest" is inspired by the following news story: Kimberly Truong, "Woman Who Climbed Statue of Liberty to Protest Family Separation Found Guilty," *The Cut*, December 18, 2018, https://www.thecut.com/2018/12/therese-patricia-okoumou-found-guilty-statue-of-liberty-climb.html.

"Watching the News in My Attorney's Waiting Room": the duplex form credited to Jericho Brown.

"I Don't Know, I Don't Know" is a found poem from Salem Witch Trials Documentary Archive and Transcription Project, http://salem.lib.virginia.edu/n63.html#n63.2. Title attributed to Donald Trump.

"The Witch Dungeon Museum" is informed by information from the following website: Witch Dungeon Museum,

Atlas Obscura, http://www.atlasobscura.com/places/witch-dungeon-museum.

"Trump Has Called the Investigation a Witch Hunt 84 Times" quotes (in italics) and inspiration are from Salem Witch Trials Documentary Archive and Transcription Project, http://salem.lib.virginia.edu/n87.html, http://salem.lib.virginia.edu/n24.html. The title was inspired by Olivia Paschal, "Trump's Tweets and the Creation of 'Illusory Truth,'" *Atlantic*, August 3, 2018, https://www.theatlantic.com/politics/archive/2018/08/how-trumps-witch-hunt-tweets-create-an-illusory-truth/566693/.

"You've Got to Deny, Deny, and Push Back on These Women" is inspired by the following news story: Jade Hayden, "Judge Quotes Bible to Justify Women's Assault by Her Ex-Husband," Her, October 24, 2018, https://www.her.ie/news/judge-quoted-bible-justify-womans-assault-ex-371815. Title attributed to Donald Trump.

"Obstruction of Justice" quotes (in italics) and inspiration from Salem Witch Trials Documentary Archive and Transcription Project, http://salem.lib.virginia.edu/n45.html.

"Taylor Swift Makes *Forbes*'s Most Powerful Women List" incorporates tweets referenced in Rachel Epstein, "Why the Internet Is Comparing Taylor Swift's Performance to a Witch Ritual," October 9, 2018, Yahoo Sports, https://sports.yahoo.com/why-internet-comparing-taylor-swift-003500248.html.

"I, Hecate" is informed by information from "Hecate," Wikipedia, accessed April 4, 2021, https://en.wikipedia.org/wiki/Hecate, and WiseWitch, "Famous Witches—Hecate," Witchcraft, http://www.witchcraftandwitches.com/witches_hecate.html.

Acknowledgments

Grateful acknowledgment is made to the following publications in which these poems, or versions of these poems, first appeared (some with different titles as noted in parentheses):

The Academy of American Poets, Poem-a-Day: "Rose of Jericho"

AGNI: "Trump Has Called the Investigation a Witch Hunt 84 Times" ("Martha Carrier")

Aunt Flo Anthology: "I, Chedipe"

Forklift, Ohio: "I Don't Know, I Don't Know" ("Sarah Good")

Ghost Bible: "Blessed Teresa of Calcutta Declared a Saint Before Huge Crowd at the Vatican," "Dear Moon"

Lily Poetry Review: "Mary of the Blessed Innocent" ("Mary Ayer Parker")

Love's Executive Order: "Ogre"

Muddy River Poetry Review: "Margaret Scott of Children Lost" ("Margaret Scott"), "Rebecca Nurse of the Accused" ("Rebecca Nurse")

New England Poetry Club: "The Witch Dungeon Museum"

Nimrod International Journal: "I Have Seen Women Manipulate Men with Just a Twitch of Their Eye" ("Factors"), "Spectral Evidence"

Nixes Mate Review: "Contradiction Express," "I, Witch," "No Collusion" ("Wilmott Redd"), "Our Lady of Perpetual Compassion" ("Ann Pudeator"), "Such a Nasty Woman" ("Susannah Martin")

North Meridian Review: "I, Circe"

Ovenbird Poetry: "He Punishes Me with Flowers"

Phantom Drift: "Oomancy Triggers Witch Hunt"

Psaltery & Lyre: "Tornado Warning"

Salamander: "Obstruction of Justice" ("Mary Easty")

Solstice Literary Magazine: "What Bird Was That"

Somerville Times: "Gallows Project Team Verifies Site of Salem Witch Trial Hangings"

SWWIM: "Spell"

Three Drops from a Cauldron: "I, Hecate," "I, Kikimora"

Timberline Review: "In Search Of"

UnLost Journal: "At the Threshold"

Washington Independent Review of Books: "Trump Has Called the Investigation a Witch Hunt 84 Times" ("Martha Carrier," reprinted from *AGNI*)

Innocents, a chapbook including some of the poems in this collection, was published by Nixes Mate Publishers in March 2020.

I would like to thank CavanKerry Press—Joan Cusack Handler, Gabriel Cleveland, Dimitri Reyes, and Baron Wormser—for bringing this book to life. I am forever grateful to my beloved poetry family: Kathi Aguero, Kevin Carey, M. P. Carver, John Harn, Richard Hoffman, Elisabeth Horowitz, Jennifer Jean, Danielle Jones, Kali Lightfoot, Jennifer Martelli, Colleen Michaels, January O'Neil, Carla Panciera, Dawn Paul, J. D. Scrimgeour, and the Salem Writers Group. Susan Rich, this book would not be what it is without your magic or your friendship. To my lifelong friends—Carol, Cynthia, Jane, and Susan B.—thank you for sticking with me through the years. Thank you to Joanne and Patty for nurturing me when I needed it most. To my brother, Carson, and sister, Cathy, thank you for being my rocks. To my children, my greatest loves, Carson and Ketner, thank you for being my reason. And, lastly, in appreciation and remembrance of my father, Carson Ward Veach—for his steadfast support, for every single fascinating conversation, for his deep insight, intelligence, humanity, and wit.

CavanKerry's Mission

A not-for-profit literary press serving art and community, CavanKerry is committed to expanding the reach of poetry and other fine literature to a general readership by publishing works that explore the emotional and psychological landscapes of everyday life, and to bringing that art to the underserved where they live, work, and receive services.

Other Books in the Emerging Voices Series

This book was printed on paper from responsible sources.

Her Kind as been set in Warnock Pro, an old-style typeface commissioned by Chris Warnock in honor of his father, John Warnock, in 1997. It was designed by Robert Slimbach and first published in 2000.